SERMON OUTLINES

on

Youth Related Issues

Charles R. Wood

kregel
PUBLICATIONS

Grand Rapids, MI 49501

Sermon Outlines on Youth Related Issues
by Charles R. Wood

© 1984 by Kregel Publications, a division of Kregel, Inc.,
P.O. Box 2607, Grand Rapids, MI 49501.

For more information about Kregel Publications, visit our
web site at: www.kregel.com

Library of Congress Cataloging-in-Publication
Sermon outlines on youth related issues / by Charles R.
Wood.
         p.   cm.
1. Youth sermons—Outlines, syllabi, etc. I. Title.
BV4310.W582   1984   252'.55—dc20   83-25543

ISBN 0-8254-4134-x

          7 8 9 10 printing / year 09 08 07 06

Printed in the United States of America

Contents

Introduction

Although it is not really true, teenagers have long been considered a "breed apart," to be approached carefully and no more often than necessary unless one is saddled with the responsibilities of parenthood or school teaching. The Pastor or Christian leader had occasionally forced contact through the weekly youth meeting, the national convention's "Youth Day" program, or an infrequent request to speak to a group of teens at a retreat or after an outing.

The rise of the Christian school movement has changed all that. Virtually every town of any size in the United States has a Christian school; and with the Christian School goes the chapel service, the special assembly and the commencement program. Increasingly, the Pastor and the Christian leader are called upon to speak to teens as a regular part of their ministry.

For the man familiar with teens, their special characteristics and unique needs, this presents no special problem. For the man who has not yet had the questionable blessing of parenthood involving teens, for the man whose own children are long grown, and for those who find being the father of a teenager even more confusing than it is made out to be, this frequent responsibility creates an entirely new set of concomitants. "What shall I talk about?" "What interests kids today?" "How can I hold their attention?" These and a host of other questions arise as one contemplates the forthcoming assignment.

Here is help!

For the past eight years the compiler of these sermons (who also originally preached these messages to teens) has been deeply involved in the Christian school movement as Pastor, teacher, and frequent chapel speaker. Each of these messages has been preached in the chapel program of a Christian school (most of them at Grace Baptist Church High School, South Bend, Indiana). Those which are presented here have been selected from among a larger number on the basis of the acceptance and good response which they evoked. Carefully studied, thought through and fleshed out with personal illustrations, they should prove interesting, stimulating and generative of response. The fact that they are intentionally and intensely practical should contribute toward their usefulness, for they are designed to be put into practice in the lives of the teens to whom they are preached. May God use them to change lives!

God's Answers to the Problems of Modern Young People

ECCLESIASTES 12:1

Introduction:

The Bible makes it clear that Christianity is for young people. Young people, however, have trouble with Christianity because of the problems they face. Most of those problems fall into a few categories, and God has the answers for them.

I.   **The Need for a Standard Conduct Is Answered by the Bible**
   A. The Bible lays down general rules for life
      1. Specific in some instances (Ten Commandments)
      2. General overall rules of conduct ("All Scripture is given by inspiration..." 2 Timothy 3:16)
   B. The Bible provides the means for keeping out of trouble ("Wherewithal shall a young man..." Psalm 119:9)
      1. Keep life in accord with the Word of God ("Thy Word have I hid..." Psalm 119:11)
      2. Get to know it better so you can know what it teaches ("Study to show thyself approved unto God..." 2 Timothy 2:15)

II. **The Need for a Place of Service (Activity) Is Answered by the Church**
   A. The church organized by Christ for purpose of worship and service
      1. Young people are to have a part in it
      2. The position of young people is regulated in the church (1 Peter 5:5)
   B. Church obligations are upon young as well as old
      1. If youth wants its place in the church, it should be willing to take its place of responsibility
      2. The church needs to provide a place for youth

III. **The Need for Self-expression Is Answered by Christian Witnessing**

A. God's command is for us to witness
   1. The Gospel is nothing to be ashamed of ("For I am not ashamed . . ." Romans 1:16)
   2. We are always to be ready to give an answer ("Be ready always to give an answer to every man that asketh you a reason for the hope that is in you with meekness and fear." 1 Peter 3:15)
B. Witnessing brings great results
   1. Eternal results ("He that winneth souls is wise." Proverbs 11:30)
   2. Temporal results (James 5:20)

IV. **The Need for Proper Motivation Is Answered by Devotion to God**
A. All things are to be done with the idea of pleasing God
   1. Positive side ("And all things . . ." 1 Corinthians 10:31)
   2. Negative side ("Let nothing be done through strife or vain glory." Philippians 2:3)
B. The approval of God will serve as the standard of motivation
   1. Whether or not a thing pleases God determines its worth
   2. The whole self should be sold out to pleasing God

V. **The Need for Security Is Answered by the Christian Home and Salvation**
A. The Christian Home
   1. God's basic unit is the family
   2. Example of parents important (Titus 2:1-8)
B. Salvation
   1. Provides present security
   2. Provides eternal security

Conclusion:
Teens have many problems, but God has the answer to them all. Those answers are found in the Word of God. It is not enough, however, to know the answers. We must take them and put them into practice in our daily lives.

Tell It Like It Is!

Introduction:

Young people have many terms which they use. Sometimes these terms are foreign to adults, but there is one that is very clear: "Tell it like it is." When it comes to teens, we do need to do that very thing. Here are some suggestions:

I.   **Tell It Like It Is About Teens**
   A. The tremendous importance of teens
     1. General individual worth
     2. Potential for future
     3. Ripeness for plucking
   B. The difficulty of working with teens
     1. Unpredictable
     2. Rowdy, raucous, rebellious
   C. The rewards of working with teens
     1. Eternal
     2. Present

II. **Tell It Like It Is to Teens**
   A. Urgency
     1. Our days are too crucial to gloss over
     2. Youth is hearing and expects to hear
   B. Content
     1. Spiritual commitment (price of Christianity)
     2. Physical well-being (drugs, alcohol, cigarettes, etc.)
     3. Morals (proper level)
   C. Methodology
     1. Can be done without preaching
     2. We ought to use best methods available
     3. Reasoned, unhypocritical answers

III. **Tell It Like It Is With Teens**
   A. Meaning
     1. Consistent living to back up teaching
     2. Boils down to practicing what is preached
   B. Reasons

   1. Charges of hypocrisy make kids more observant than ever
   2. Freedom really to present the truth
   3. Tremendous power of example
  C. Urgency
   1. Only positive influence some teens have
   2. Darkness of the hour demands brightness of life

IV. Tell It Like It Is for (in behalf of) Teens
  A. Desperate need for workers
   1. Many who will, can not; who can, will not
   2. Need is for dedicated, qualified workers
   3. Must see importance of work with teens
  B. The type of work needed
   1. Established priorities
   2. Full dedication of self and effort
   3. Willingness to sacrifice
  C. The appeal involved
   1. See the importance of teens
   2. See the necessity of quality
   3. Give yourself to it

Conclusion:
 This is a message which has tried to "tell it like it is." How is it with you? Can you "tell it like it is" because you know it like it is?

The Christian Teen and the $3 Bill

Introduction:
Most Christian teens are not nearly as bad as older people think nor nearly as good as they try to look. No one knows teens half as well as other teens. $3 bills are rejected in most areas of life. Unfortunately, Christian teens are not as wise in determining what to accept and what to reject.

I.   **Who Is a Phony?**
   A. The conformist
   B. The quiet rebel
   C. The outright hypocrite
   D. The one who agrees and violates
   E. The play actor

II.   **Why Are There Phonies?**
   A. Weak people who want to do better
   B. Those who don't want a "hassle"
   C. Those who are blind to their own problems
   D. Those who are "chicken"
   E. Those who are deliberately dishonest

III.   **What Are the Dangers?**
   A. Divided mind — makes one continuously restless
   B. Wrong actions follow wrong thoughts
   C. God's knowledge — He knows whether or not you are real
   D. Exposure — "Be sure your sin will find you out" (Numbers 32:23).
   E. Judgment — God will act in time
   F. Damage to self (many an adult has no self-respect because of patterns of phoniness)

IV.   **What Is the Answer?**
   A. Submission to God's authority
   B. Bring actions and thoughts into line

      1. Don't start acting rebellious
      2. Begin to think and believe what you act
  C. Seek God's help

Conclusion:

No thinking teen would accept a $3 bill for change in the school cafeteria. God will no more accept our phony stuff than we will accept the $3 bill. It is time for the phony to become genuine.

Watch Your Attitude

1 SAMUEL 16:7

Introduction:
An attitude is a hard thing to define. Most parents say, "Watch your attitude," but they do not really get specific. An attitude is a mind-set, true inner view, inner response. It is tremendously important as it often spells the difference between success and failure, happiness and unhappiness, trouble and liberated living.

I. **Learning**
   A. You are here to learn — not to teach
   B. Forget your preconceptions
   C. Evaluate rather than vocalize

II. **Obedience**
   A. Definition: Doing what one is told to do, when told to do it and with a right spirit
   B. It is better to obey, even with a strong spirit, than it is not to obey
   C. It is better by far to do so with a right spirit
   D. Learn to obey and to do so willingly

III. **Submission**
   A. Akin to obedience
   B. The nature of the submissive spirit
      1. Place yourself under those in authority
      2. Seek opportunities to submit
      3. God does not give us authority until we learn to submit to the authority of others

IV. **Co-operation**
   A. Seek opportunities to work with others
   B. This involves much selflessness

V. **Contentment**
   A. There are so many reasons to be dissatisfied
   B. "Godliness with contentment is great gain"
   C. When things go bad, get used to it; they may get worse

VI. Compassion
   A. An inner concern for others
   B. Ability to spot needs and move to meet them
   C. A focus on others

VII. Commitment
   A. Giving everything your best
   B. Forget the "cool" that never commits or gets involved
   C. Get involved in the right that is going on around you

Conclusion:
   What can you do about an attitude problem?
   Confess it as sin
   Make a decision of your will regarding it
   Make positive choices and set positive goals
   We tend to act as we feel, but conscious proper actions can change the way we feel.

The God of New Beginnings

GENESIS 25:27-35

Introduction:

Sometimes life gets so mixed up that there seems to be no way to get things straightened out. It seems as if it would just be best to go back to the beginning and start over. God does make provision for such new beginnings, and He gives us a very instructive example in the life of Jacob.

I.   **The Life of Jacob Shows New Beginnings**
    A. Trace the story
        1. Purchase of birthright (Genesis 25)
        2. Theft of blessing (Genesis 27)
        3. Stop at Bethel — experience with God (28:10-15)
        4. Marriage (Genesis 29)
        5. Family growth (Genesis 30)
        6. Departure from Laban (Genesis 30, 31)
        7. Return to Bethel (32:9-12)
        8. Reconciliation to Esau (Genesis 33)
        9. Family problems (Genesis 34)
      10. Back again to Bethel (35:9)
    B. Story of change
        1. From trickster and thief to godly man
        2. From rebel to prince of God
    C. The role of Bethel
        1. The place of special meeting with God
        2. Each return marked a new beginning
        3. He came back to where he had been before

II. **The Meaning of This**
    A. God always wants our fellowship
        1. We often break it
        2. He stands waiting for our return
    B. God allows us several — many — returns
        1. His concern is to have us back
        2. He is always willing
        3. We all stray and need to come back

III. **Practical Applications**
   A. Now a new year
      1. Last year is gone
      2. Summer is over
   B. Things need to be made right with God
      1. Conditions of new beginning
         a. Confession
         b. Forsaking
      2. Forget about punishment. Getting right is important.
   C. You can get a new start
      1. Devotions
      2. Attitude (avoid rebellion)
      3. Spirit
      4. Cooperation
      5. Participation

Conclusion:

Today is like a clean slate.

The things you blamed for all your problems in the past are no longer present.

God has given you a new beginning.

What will you do with the opportunity for a new beginning which God has given you?

When Friction Is Right

1 TIMOTHY 5:20

Introduction:
Most of the time friction and trouble are to be avoided. They are usually harmful and the result of sinful pride or some other improper attitude or conduct. There are times, however, when trouble is not only right but actually necessary. This passage teaches us some "constructive troublemaking."

I. **The Word Says to Rebuke Sin — 1 Timothy 5:20**
   A. A clear command
   B. Possibly it means also to mention names
   C. Designed to warn others and to stop sinning
   D. Necessary today

II. **The Sin That Is to Be Rebuked**
   A. Sin common to all teens (e.g., sex, drugs, rebellion)
   B. Sin common to Christian teens
      1. Lying, cheating, stealing
      2. Participating in the rock culture

III. **We Must Mark Such Sinners — Romans 16:17, 18**
   A. We are to identify those who sin
   B. We are to avoid them
      1. Should stay away from them
      2. Should stay away from those who run with them
   C. This runs contrary to what we do, but it is the Bible's way

IV. **We Should Make Some Differences — Jude 22, 23**
   A. Some are rebels
      1. We should isolate them
      2. We should avoid them
   B. Some are weak
      1. Pulled toward the rebels
      2. We should pull them away from the rebels

Conclusion:

There is a certain amount of friction which is the result of doing things God's way. Try to avoid all the friction you can, but when it comes because you have done things God's way, try to keep a proper shift and learn what you can from it.

Maybe I Can Help You!

PHILIPPIANS 2:4

Introduction:
Did you ever feel completely helpless? Like no one could understand or help you with your problem no matter what? Everyone feels that way at times, but it really is not true. Maybe I can help you by showing you the cause of and cure for many of your problems.

I.   **What Is Your Problem?**
      A. Depression
      B. Bitterness
      C. Turned-off
      D. Unhappy in general

II.   **What Your Problem Really Is**
      A. Self-focus
         1. Excessive concern with self
         2. Inability to see anyone/anything else
      B. This leads to misery
         1. Keeps attention focused on needs, lacks, problems
         2. Creates a "misery cycle"

III. **The Solution to Your Problem**
      A. Get your eyes off yourself
      B. Get someone else in focus as your main concern
         1. Select someone with needs
         2. Select someone with problems greater than yours
      C. Make a project
         1. Select one person
         2. Select one thing to do for that person each day

Conclusion:
You can be miserable or you can be happy
The choice is yours
You can have it your way, or you can have it God's way

The Best Day of Your Life

PSALM 90:9-12

Introduction:
Life consists of the past, the present and the future. Most people either live in the past through regret or in the future through wishful thinking. The only day we can really live is to-day, and it is a shame to let the regrets of the past or the dreams of the future keep us from making today the best day of our lives — the only day we can really live.

I.   **The Misunderstanding of Today**
     A. Today is the tomorrow you worried about yesterday
     B. Today is the yesterday you will regret tomorrow

II. **The Importance of Today**
     A. Today is all you have
        1. You can not change yesterday
        2. You can not guarantee tomorrow
     B. Today is the first day of the rest of your life
     C. Today is the only day you can do anything about

III. **The Use of Today**
     A. Learn yesterday's lessons and forget about yesterday
     B. Plan but do not live for tomorrow
     C. Use today for all it is worth
        1. Thank God for it
        2. Enjoy it
        3. Use every bit of it
        4. Do the best you can with it
        5. Take all its responsibilities
        6. Grasp all its opportunities
        7. Do not hold back from it
        8. Live as one who will give account for it

Conclusion:
Some teens are only half living
Some are wishing life away
Today is what you have. Take it, use it, love it, cherish it
Today is the best day you have ever lived

How to Control Your Environment

PHILIPPIANS 4:11

Introduction:
Many teens have very bad home environments with which to contend. Many spend much time wishing that conditions were better. Most are not aware that something can be done about a bad environment. Even fewer have any idea of what to do with a bad situation. Here are some suggestions:

I. **You and Your Environment**
   A. Your environment is everything around you
      1. Includes all kinds of things
      2. Includes all the people in your life
   B. Your environment affects you
      1. It has considerable effect
      2. But does not have control over you

II. **You Can Make Your Own Environment**
   A. You can change some things
      1. You must change what you can
      2. You must change the way you react to such things
   B. You can change some people
      1. You must realize the possibility
      2. You must change the way you react to them

III. **How to Make Your Own Environment**
   A. Resolve to change what you can
      1. Physical surroundings
      2. New friends
   B. Resolve not to let what you can not change dominate you
   C. Specific suggestions
      1. Be friendly to everyone
      2. Participate in everything
      3. Reach out to others' needs
      4. Do something nice for someone each day
      5. Smile and be pleasant
      6. Be interested in others
      7. Act enthusiastic
      8. Stop thinking so much about yourself!

IV. **The Rewards of Making Your Own Environment**
   A. Feel better in general
   B. Be better received and liked
   C. Live in a happy atmosphere

Conclusion:
   You do not have to be dominated by the circumstances of life under which you live. You can do something about them. The question is: What will you do with your environment?

How to Handle a Bad Environment

1 CORINTHIANS 6:9-11

Introduction:
In a society as messed up as today's, it is inevitable that many young people are going to face bad situations, especially at home. Here are some thoughts which are designed to help those in bad situations rise above those situations and master their circumstances.

I. **Important Truths**
    A. You are not responsible for the mess things are in (do not let it be blamed on you!!!)
    B. You are not condemned by the situation
    C. You do not have to reproduce it (in your own life or that of your children)
    D. A bad situation may be good — part of God's plan to make something special

II. **Helpful Pointers**
    A. Stay strong in the Word of God
    B. Pray daily for strength and help
    C. Be what *you* should be (your parents' poor conduct is no excuse)
    D. Do not be judgmental of others
    E. Do not talk too much about it (especially to your friends)
    F. Keep a thankful spirit (God is doing something in and through it)
    G. Get yourself a hero (someone to whom you can look to do right)
    H. Seek godly counsel wherever it is possible
    I. Do not dwell on your problems (or use them to gain sympathy)
    J. Expect God to do something for you

Conclusion:
You really can not help where you are. You can help both what you are and what you become. Stay where you are unless there is serious physical danger. Expect some daily miracles.

How to Get What You Want

PROVERBS 18:24

Introduction:
Everyone wants something. What do you want? Is it happiness, friends, popularity, success? Here's how you can get what you want and do it in a way that honors the Lord.

I.   **You Do Not Get What You Want by Going After It!**
    A. Some things can not be gained by going after them
    B. True worthwhile things defy direct assault
       1. There are few exceptions
       2. Most exceptions turn to dust

II. **You Get What You Want by:**
    A. Being what you should be
    B. Losing yourself in a cause
    C. Following the path of duty
    D. Giving yourself away

III. **This Is Shown by Practical Examples**
    A. You become a friend to have friends ("A man that hath friends must show himself friendly")
    B. You love to be loved
    C. You do right to be satisfied
    D. You follow the path of duty to happiness ("Happiness is not a destination; it is a by-product of the journey")

Conclusion:
Some are miserable because they are all tied up in themselves. They are trying to get the things they think would make them happy (and which possibly would), but they are going about it the wrong way.

By the way — you do not even get to be spiritual just by talking. You get it by obeying.

How to Find God's Will for Your Life

JOHN 7:17

Introduction:

In a period of three or four years right at the end of the teen years, most young people will face several of the most crucial questions of life: Should I go to college? Which college should I attend? What career should I pursue? Whom shall I marry? How can you know what to do? How can you be sure of God's will? Here are a number of suggestions.

I.   **Be Sure You Know What to Do:**
  A. God does not give His will on approval
  B. The one who wills to do His will gets to know it
  C. Complete surrender is necessary

II. **Look First to Your Authorities**
  A. You are under authority until marriage
  B. Establish who your authority really is (parents, pastor, teacher)
  C. God will then mediate His will through your authorities
  D. Listen even if you completely disagree (unless your authority violates the Bible)
  E. Especially listen and obey where your authority is Christian

III. **Then Look to Other Areas**
  A. Word of God
  B. Prayer
  C. Trend of circumstance

IV. **Specific Tips**
  A. When in doubt — play safe (do not do what you are not sure you should do)
  B. Do not expect to know more than you need to know (You do not need to know today what you will be doing one year from now)
  C. The closer you walk to the Lord, the more likely you are to know what He wants for you

D. The will of God never conflicts with the Word of God
E. Do what you know to do now — the rest will open up later (We often miss the will of God for *today* because we are worrying about the will of God for the future.)

Conclusion:

God's will is not some great mystery. It can be really known by a young person. The source of it is the Bible. The key to knowing it is the willingness to do it.

•

How to Get Ahead in Life

Introduction:

Many teens want to get ahead in life — they want to be leaders, popular, successful — but so many go about it the wrong way. Clowning, arrogance, attention seeking, emphasis on self, etc., are all common methods of trying to get ahead, but all are wrong. The Bible has a program that shows how to do it.

I. **Hard Work (v. 19)**
    A. The "breaks" go to those who make them
    B. This offers a special opportunity as there are so few who work today

II. **Faithfulness (v. 20)**
    A. Similar to dependability
    B. Also includes loyalty
    C. Covers all possible areas of life

III. **Do Not Have Respect of Persons (v. 21)**
    A. People have worth and are not to be used
    B. Do not try to climb up by stepping on others
    C. Remember: the elite usually is not

IV. **Put Low Priority on Riches (v. 22)**
    A. Do not make money your goal; let it be a by-product
    B. Money is not the mark of success
    C. Ill-gotten gain will ruin

V. **Trust in the Lord (v. 25)**
    A. Believe Him enough to obey Him
    B. He can make you prosper
    C. He honors those who honor Him

IV. **Give to the Poor (v. 27)**
    A. Care for those in need
    B. This is the opposite of respect of persons
    C. You can not really give to the poor — it is a loan to the Lord

Conclusion:

Most everyone, including teens, wants to get ahead. Almost everyone tries to get ahead the wrong way. God has a right way to do it, and we ought to do it His way.

How to Live at Peace With Others

PROVERBS 3:27-32

Introduction:
It is common for there to be friction between Christian teens. Sometimes a youth group or school is torn by that trouble. It surely is unnecessary to have most of the troubles that exist, because the Word of God is very clear on how to live at peace with others. This brief passage contains four specific steps.

I. **Withhold Not (vv. 27, 28)**
    A. Command
       1. "Withhold not good"
       2. Do not postpone meeting a neighbor's needs
    B. Conditions
       1. "When it is in the power of your hand to do it" (when you have it by you)
       2. Those "to whom it is due." (We are not to help just anyone)
    C. Clarification
       1. Based on concept of mutual responsibility as Christians
       2. Based on "giving-living" concepts (We give to get to give again)

II. **Scheme Not (v. 29)**
    A. Do not become involved in evil plots against a neighbor
    B. Especially avoid becoming involved in something evil against someone who has confidence in you

III. **Strive Not (v. 30)**
    A. Caution
       1. Do not strive when there is no just cause (Do not "pick a fight")
       2. Do not strive against the man who has done nothing to you worthy of strife
    B. Corrective
       1. Strife itself is not necessarily wrong
       2. The cause and issue of the strife are the main factors

29

IV. **Envy Not (vv. 31, 32)**
    A. The object (v. 31)
       1. The oppressor — the one who gets ahead by putting down other people
       2. The oppressor's ways — they appear good because they tend to work
    B. The obvious (v. 32)
       1. The perverse is an abomination to the Lord
       2. The secret of the Lord is with the righteous

Conclusion:
Living at peace with others is simpler than it often appears. There are certain basic principles which when applied will create that situation of peace. The peace they bring is worth the effort.

How to Get Along With Others

PROVERBS 3:28, 29

Introduction:

Teens can be terrors, and the best of friends one day can be at odds with each other the next. Adults often learn how to put differences aside and get along with each other, but teens seldom do. Here are seven simple steps on how to get along with others.

I. **Do Not Devise Evil Against Anyone (v. 28)**
    A. Do not be party to hurtful horse-play
    B. Do not gang up on others
    C. Do not participate in planned snubs

II. **Do Not Strive Without a Cause (v. 29)**
    A. Do not be belligerent
    B. Do not pick on others
    C. Do not be overbearing

III. **Do Not Force Yourself on Others**
    A. Do not let critics call your shots by forcing you to do what they want
    B. Do not allow people to set your course by yielding to the pressure they put on you

IV. **Do Not Brag Idly**
    A. Do not boast of the wrong you have done
    B. It alienates people from you
    C. It impresses the wrong kind of people

V. **Do Face Issues (Proverbs 27:6)**
    A. A true friend is helpful
    B. A person who never disagrees is likely not a friend

VI. **Do Show Yourself Friendly (Proverbs 18:24)**
    A. Be to others what you would like them to be to you
    B. Go out of your way for people
    C. Be more concerned with others than with yourself

VII. Do Be Available
A. Avoid exclusive friendships
B. Be aware of the needs of others

Conclusion:
If you are having trouble making friends or getting along with people, it would be wise to check the principles before blaming an "unfriendly" group of teens or looking for some individual "scapegoat".

How to Be Strong

JAMES 1:2-5

Introduction:

Almost everyone admires a truly strong person. Almost everyone wants to be successful in life. Most of the successful people in life are strong people. How can I be strong and successful as a result? Here's a biblical program.

I.   **The Quest for Strength**
   A. False conceptions
      1. Comes by acting strong
      2. Comes by magic
      3. Comes by picking it up out of the air
   B. Failed understanding
      1. We want to be strong, but we do not want to do what it takes
      2. We fail to see how things connect (cause/effect relationships)

II. **The Source of Strength**
   A. In the natural world
      1. Strength comes from the hard work of development
      2. Strength comes from repeated success in difficult things
   B. Spiritual strength comes same way
      1. We grow through the hard things
      2. James says that spiritual strength comes through diligent effort in the midst of trials

III. **The Lessons of Strength**
   A. We always want the easy way
      1. Complain about the hard
      2. Quit the difficult
      3. Grasp for the easy
   B. We should be seeking the difficult
      1. Be glad if your parents are tough

2. Appreciate the difficult teacher (get priorities off grades and on learning)
3. Tackle the thing that is hard for you to do

Conclusion:

Success will not always be determined by ability (some less able will be more successful than many more able). As much as anything, your ability to handle the difficult things and situations in life will determine the measure of your success.

Steps to Strength

EPHESIANS 6:10

Introduction:
There are many weaklings among teens, but most of them wish they were not. Many want to grow stronger but simply do not know how to go about it. Here are seven steps to strength that will work for a teen, who really wants to be strong.

I.   Settle the Issue That the Only Real Strength Is in Christ

II.   Accept the Terms of Bible Obedience
    A. God gives steps to strength
    B. In obedience, we find a sense of well-being
    C. Obedience removes guilt and the need to cover up

III. Decide to Do Things God's Way
    A. As contrasted with your way
    B. Only His way will work

IV. Try Doing Devotions Rather Than Having Devotions
    A. Put the Bible into practice in life
    B. Let your devotions continue throughout the whole day

V.   Seek Counsel in Weak Areas
    A. Turn to someone who can help
    B. Stay away from those who have the same weaknesses you have, for they cannot help you

VI. Find a Good Example, and Pattern After Him/Her
    A. Someone who is strong
    B. It can be an adult or another teen

VII. Develop Specific Projects to Work on
    A. Make yourself a promise concerning an area of weakness
    B. Two suggestions:
       1. Work on keeping quiet
       2. Get some new friends who are strong

Conclusion:

If you want to be strong — and who does not — then here are the steps to strength. Now it is up to you to develop your strength according to biblical principles.

What to Do When You
Do Not Know What to Do

PROVERBS 3:5, 6

Introduction:
We are so often faced with things for which we are not
equipped or with decisions which we are not ready to make. The
pressures of life become so great that we get confused. We say,
"I don't know what to do." This is what to do when you don't
know what to do.

I. **Walk Closely With the Lord**
   A. Daily fellowship maintained with Him will help in
      time of need.
   B. Make regular practice of turning everything over to
      Him

II. **Take the Matter to Him in Prayer**
   A. Do not ever do anything without His guidance
   B. Do not fail to do anything He shows you

III. **Do Not Try to Figure Things Out on Your Own — "Lean
      not on your own understanding"**
   A. Unaided reason will always lead to more problems
   B. It is not wrong to use your reason
      1. Not your reason *alone*
      2. Reason must be submitted to the will of God

IV. **Submit Self and Situation to His Will**
   A. Be willing no matter what His will may be ("If any
      man will do His will, he shall know of the doctrine."
      John 7:17)
   B. Do not try to predetermine or "rubber-stamp" His
      will

V. **Clearly Express Your Problem**
   A. Put it in writing
      1. It helps to clarify it
      2. Sometimes we find answers while stating the
         problem

B. Be sure you really have a problem
   1. Sometimes our only problem is worry
   2. Some problems are not worth having

VI. **Search for Bible Principles**
     A. If no direct teaching available
     B. Try to find principles that apply
        1. Why it is important to express the problem clearly
        2. There are principles for every situation

VII. **Be Sure There Is No Sin Or Disobedience Involved**
     A. "If I regard iniquity in my heart. . ." (Psalm 66:18)
     B. Sin blocks
        1. Not doing what we know while seeking to know more
        2. Broken fellowship prevents answers
     C. Sometimes our problem is that we know the answer but just will not act on it

VIII. **Seek Godly Counsel**
      A. Cautions
         1. Do not go to those you know will agree with you
         2. Do not seek too many
         3. Use wisdom in determining to whom you go
      B. Why it helps
         1. Others may have been through the same experience
         2. The uninvolved see more clearly

IX. **Do Not Act Until You Have to Or Until You Know What to Do**
     A. Many times we do not have answers because we do not need them at this time
     B. Many situations care for themselves or provide their own answers

X.   **Expect God to Give You Direction**
     A. Move on — don't let it tie you up
     B. This is a promise

Conclusion:
   There are always times when you simply do not know what to do about a situation or a decision. Here are some steps to take when you do not know what to do. These steps can help you to do something about the tough situations of life.

What to Do With a Bad Report Card

Introduction:
What would I do with a bad report card?

I would resolve that it would be the last one I would ever get, and then I would go to work on that resolve.

I. **Some Suggestions**
  A. First thought
    1. Lose it
    2. Burn it
    3. Throw it down the sewer
    4. Sign it yourself and bring it back
  B. Second thought
    1. Blame the teachers — "She gave me" (If you really feel you were given what you did not earn — see the teacher)
    2. Say the school, class, or teacher is too hard
    3. Say everyone is down on you — (If they are, you probably earned it)
  C. Third thought
    1. What difference does it make — just be casual about it
    2. Make a big joke of it — all the world loves a clown, except employers
    3. Give up — why try when you can not do better than that
    4. Quit school — what is the point of it anyhow?

II. **Some Better Ideas**
  A. Take it as a warning
    1. Lack of background in a subject (s)
    2. Failure to study
    3. Not bothering to do homework
  B. Realize it is not fatal
    1. Grades can be pulled up
    2. You likely can still pass for the semester or year
  C. Quit the nonsense
    1. You do not *have* to be absent that much

      2. Try listening in class
      3. Do some homework for a change
      4. How about a bit of studying?
      5. Stop the fussing and excuse-making
      6. A little less clowning, please
  D. Get busy
      1. You can still bring it up to passing (without miracles)
      2. Work is necessary — some work which might make you a success in life in general
      3. Set some goals
      4. Get to where you can ask the Lord to help you

Conclusion:

What would I do with a bad report card? I would resolve that it would be the last one I would ever get, and then I would go to work on that resolve.

Disorderly Conduct

2 THESSALONIANS 3:6

Introduction:
There are some Christian teens who will not do things God's way no matter what. They are clearly described in God's Word, and we are very specifically told what to do about them.
Who is involved:

I. **Brothers That Walk Disorderly**
   A. Does not refer to the loud, etc.
   B. Means — those who do not walk according to the Word
      1. Rebels
      2. Unspiritual
      3. Those who do not practice biblical living
      4. Those who reject authority

II. **Withdraw Yourself**
   A. Get away from them
      1. Isolate them
      2. Cut off fellowship with them
   B. This is a commandment!!!
      1. We do not have the option
      2. Note strengthening of the commandment in the passage
   C. Runs counter of our usual reasoning
      1. "Someone has to be a friend to them"
      2. We have to win them back
   D. God's purpose
      1. Isolate
      2. Bring them back to fellowship through isolation

III. **What It Means**
   A. Watch out for some
      1. Those who do not do it God's way
      2. Get a "mark" on them
   B. Isolate them
   C. Let God handle the rest of it

Conclusion:
We are always involved in trying to do God's work for Him. If you would stop intervening in the things God is doing in the lives of rebels, etc., He might be able to accomplish what He is doing.

Hotdogs and Heroes

COLOSSIANS 4:6; TITUS 2:8a

Introduction:
God's Word makes it very clear how we are to live, but living according to the Word can also cause us some problems. We need to balance biblical principles to avoid trouble.

I. **Problem Faced**
    A. The Bible does not allow retaliation
    B. Some take advantage of that
       1. Ridicule and harass
       2. They hide behind rules
    C. Other teens think these "hotdogs" are "heroes"

II. **Problem Explored**
    A. Two kinds of people: the strong and the weak
    B. Two kinds of weak people
       1. The inept and incompetent
       2. The loudmouthed compensators
    C. Genuinely strong people do not say much about it — they just act
    D. This creates confusion
       1. Loudmouths appear strong, when they are actually weak
       2. The strong sometimes appear weak
    E. Undiscerning teens can not sort out the difference

III. **Problem Faced**
    A. To the "hotdogs"
       1. Your weakness is showing
       2. The Bible does not allow retaliation, but the strong might lose control!
    B. To the stronger
       1. Keep control
       2. Do not retaliate
    C. Others
       1. Do not make heroes out of "hotdogs"
       2. Do not be drawn to losers

Conclusion:

It takes some discernment to determine who is a "hot-dog" and who is a genuine hero. A little study of the Bible and some prayerful thought would go a long way toward helping you to tell the difference and avoid the trouble that can come from failing to discern.

When Things Go Badly

PSALM 27:5

Introduction:
We all have bad days. It makes us feel a bit better when we observe that others have bad days as well, but that fact really does not do us any good. There are ways of handling them that can turn them into good days.

I. **Sense That God Is Speaking**
   A. May be punishment
   B. May be trying to get your attention
   C. May be trying to do something in your life
   D. May be trying to teach patience

II. **Ask God to Make His Message Clear**
   A. Spend time in prayer
   B. Spend time in His Word
   C. Seek counsel

III. **Be Willing to Learn**
   A. Act on what He shows
   B. Shorten the time of suffering by changing what needs changing

IV. **Do Not Run From Trouble**
   A. Literally — you can not get away from what God is doing
   B. Figuratively — by trying to quit, cop-out, blame-shift, etc.

V. **Let Trials Make You What You Should Be**
   A. No one ever became great without great trials
   B. Learn the lessons God has for you in them

Conclusion:
Even when things go badly, God is working in your situation. Look for the bright side, because what God does, makes, or allows has some good thing in it for you that you might miss if you do not look for it.

The Way of the Transgressor

PROVERBS 13:15

Introduction:
The Bible is a very realistic book. It not only points out how things should be, but it also clearly shows how things really are — sometimes other than they should be, as the teaching of this verse indicates.

I. **Who Is the Transgressor?**
   A. Anyone who does things any way other than God's
   B. Includes many people
      1. The immoral person — in any manner
      2. The law breaker — especially of God's Law
      3. The rebel

II. **What Is the Hard Way?**
   A. It is already hard
   B. How is it hard?
      1. Uncomfortable
      2. Miserable
      3. Filled with problems
   C. Why is it hard?
      1. Because the person on it is not following directions
      2. God will not allow anything else
         a. He can not allow competition
         b. He wants each person in His way

III. **What Should Be Done?**
   A. We must recognize that no other way will work
   B. We must stop making excuses
      1. Poor self-concept
      2. Bad home environment
      3. Inadequate parents
      4. Other people lead me astray
   C. We must make a commitment to change

Conclusion:
God said it — I believe it. I will not try to do differently. Anyone who does lives dangerously, because, "He that hardeneth his neck..." He probably will not be killed; something worse will happen.

What Kind Are You?

1 THESSALONIANS 5:14

Introduction:
   Most people have a very good idea of what a rebel is like and could probably spot one like that from a great distance. Unfortunately, not all rebels are typical. There are several kinds, and it is good to be able to recognize each of them.

I. **The Open, Hostile Rebel**
    A. He is the kind just described
    B. He is always recognized

II. **The Quiet Rebel**
    A. He never says much
    B. He resists by
       1. Refusing to act
       2. Failing to act

III. **The Passive Rebel ("chicken")**
    A. He does not really resist
    B. He does what is expected
       1. He has no heart in it
       2. He "bad mouths" it all the time he is doing it

IV. **The Conformist Rebel**
    A. He goes along with everything
    B. He rarely gets into trouble
       1. He hates every minute of it
       2. He builds up to blow-up (he is even capable of murder)

V. **The Vicarious Rebel**
    A. He does not show rebellion
    B. He is drawn to those who show rebellion
       1. He shows rebellion through others
       2. He is amused by others' rebellion

Conclusion:
Who is a rebel? A person who will not accept the authority of others in his life. Not all rebels, however, are open. There are many other kinds as well. What kind are you?

Authority

ROMANS 13:1

Introduction:

There are few things more difficult for most teens than taking orders from an authority of any kind. It just cuts against the grain of fleshly rebellion and youthful exuberance. It is, however, very important for teens to understand authority and its structure.

I.   **The Basis of Authority**
   A. God is sovereign
   B. He has established all lesser authorities
   C. He has given a "chain of command"

II. **The Nature of Authority**
   A. It covers all areas of life (God's will)
   B. It moves in specific chains
   C. It is designed to keep order
   D. It moves by progression through various stages

III. **The Reason for Authority**
   A. It prevents anarchy
   B. It allows older to lead on the basis of experience
   C. It restrains human rebellion
   D. It teaches us to submit to Him (as we submit to others)

IV. **The Limits of Authority**
   A. It stays within the confines of chain (your parents, mate, etc.)
   B. It is always limited by the Word of God
   C. Beyond those qualifications, it is always total
   D. You will never be called into account for obeying (unless you have violated a biblical principle in so doing)

Conclusion:

Every disobedience has a price in all of life. In everything we do we are sowing and reaping. How are you doing at sowing? It will determine what you reap in the future.

The Perils of Pauline
(or How to Survive in a Small Youth Group or Christian School)

Introduction:
Many Christian schools are small. Small schools have a number of problems all their own. Here are some tips for surviving in the small school.

I.   **Mind Your Own Business**
    A. Allow others a personal life
    B. Do not ask too many questions

II. **Keep Your Own Counsel**
    A. Do not tell all you know
    B. Realize that what you tell others (even in confidence) will spread

III. **Stop the Gossip**
    A. Definition
        1. Things that are untrue
        2. Things are true, but
            a. Hurtful to the person
            b. None of your business
    B. Resolve not to be a carrier
    C. Reprove it in others

IV. **Get Your Feelings off Your Shoulder**
    A. Ask God for help
    B. Give your expectations to Him
    C. Grow up a bit

V.   **Do Not Take Yourself Too Seriously**
    A. The world does not end with one disappointment
    B. You are not the center of the universe

VI. **Seek a Servant's Heart**
    A. Try to serve others
    B. This does not involve
        1. Probing someone's private life
        2. Trying to right their wrongs

Conclusion:

You can survive in a small Christian school (or any other small setting for that matter). In fact, you can actually benefit from it. You can grow up spiritually and emotionally. It is entirely up to you to determine what you will do.

Freedom

JOHN 8:31, 32

Introduction:
Everyone wants freedom. Something inside us seems to struggle for it. The tragedy is that teens often want something that really is not freedom, because they do not understand the real nature of freedom. Here are thoughts to help you to understand.

I.   **The Usual Approach to Freedom**
    A. Get rid of restraints (parents, authorities, government)
    B. Do your own thing (whatever you want, you can do)

II.   **The Bible's Approach**
    A. "The truth shall make you free" (John 8:32)
       1. Statement of fact
       2. Truth is the real way to freedom
    B. We must know the truth
       1. Truth is the Bible (John 17:17)
       2. Knowing the Bible leads to knowing the truth
    C. Freedom comes by *knowing* the Bible
       1. Real knowledge involves action
       2. Knowing without doing involves folly and not freedom
    D. *Living* by the Bible leads to freedom

III. **The Logical Proof**
    A. Created products do not decide to "do their own thing"
    B. Things do not decide to be used for a purpose other than that for which there were created
    C. A train is most free, when it is running on its track

Conclusion:
Everyone wants to be free, but there is only one way to be free. You can do things God's way and know freedom, or you can do it your own way and live in bondage. Which course will you choose?

Things My Father Taught Me

PROVERBS 1:1-6

Introduction:
   Most teens are not especially close to their parents. It is often the mature years that bring realization of just how much a parent was teaching during the growing-up years. Here is one adult's evaluation of the things his father taught him.

I.   **You Can Do Anything You Really Want to Do**
      A. Within human limits, of course
      B. "I'd give anything" — no, you would not
      C. We live within our own set of limitations

II.   **If It's Worth Doing At All, It's Worth Doing Well**
      A. If we can not give something all we have, we should not be doing it
      B. The Christian should strive for excellence
      C. Ban the half-hearted and blast the mediocrity

III. **The Will of God Is the Most Important Thing in Life**
      A. There is no substitute for being where God wants you to be
      B. Do everything possible
         1. To discern His will
         2. To do His will

IV.   **If the Bible Says It, Do It!**
      A. This assumes
         1. The inspiration of the Bible
         2. The authority of the Bible
      B. Does not allow for us to explain it away
      C. Biblical obedience is so crucial and yet so lacking

V.   **There Is Nothing Greater Than Salvation**
      A. Explain salvation
      B. It is absolutely essential because of eternity

Conclusion:
   The things my father taught me seemed rather insignificant at the time, but they have helped me tremendously throughout life. Have you learned them yet?

Fatherly Advice

PROVERBS 4

Introduction:
This chapter is filled with small tidbits of instruction from a father to his son. The qualifications of the father to teach were given in verses 1-4. They are basically that he can teach his son because he, himself, was taught by a wise father.

I.   **Get Wisdom and Understanding (vv. 5-9)**
    A. Key verse (v. 7)
        1. Wisdom is the most important and best thing to get
        2. Along with wisdom, be sure to get understanding
    B. Detailed benefits
        1. Preservations (v. 6)
            a. From folly
            b. From harm and danger
        2. Promotion (v. 8)
            a. Careful attention to wisdom will result in you becoming the kind of man who can be promoted
            b. Wisdom acted upon brings one to a place of honor
        3. Prosperity (v. 9)
            a. A crown of grace for your head
            b. A crown of glory on your life

II.   **Hear and Heed My Sayings (10-13; 20-22)**
    A. Key verse (v. 13)
        1. Grasp instruction in a way that it will not escape
        2. Keep hold of her, for she is crucial to life
    B. Benefits
        1. The years of your life shall be many (v. 10)
            a. You will avoid the errors that could cost you your life from illness or injury
            b. You will avoid things for which God might have to chasten you
        2. Your pathway will be unimpeded (v. 12)
            a. No hindrance in the pathway of life
            b. Even haste shall not be hindered

C. Background — the one teaching urges this, because he is sure his teaching is correct (v. 11)
D. Ramifications (vv. 20-22)
   1. Listen (v. 20)
   2. Heed (v. 21)
   3. Benefit (v. 22)

III. **Avoid the Way of the Wicked (vv. 14-19)**
   A. Commandment (vv. 14, 15)
      1. Stay away from the wicked and the path they walk
      2. A strong statement in four-fold prohibition
   B. Caution (vv. 16, 17)
      1. They find no rest unless they have done something to someone
      2. Even their bread and wine (the regular course of their lives) is tainted with violence
   C. Contrast (vv. 18, 19)
      1. The path of the just grows brighter until it reaches the perfect day (v. 18)
      2. The way of the wicked is dark, becomes darker, and leads to an ultimate fall (v. 19)

IV. **Live Life Carefully (vv. 23-27)**
   A. Keep thy heart (v. 23)
      1. Be diligent with thine heart
      2. The issues of life come out of your heart
   B. Keep thy lips (v. 24)
      1. Put away a crooked (double-talking) mouth
      2. Put perverse (perverted) lips far from thee
   C. Keep thy eyes (v. 25)
      1. Let them look straight before thee
      2. Make them refrain from looking at what they should not see
   D. Keep thy feet (vv. 26, 27)
      1. Consider the places you allow your feet to go
      2. Make sure all your ways are thought out
      3. Do not turn aside from the proper path
      4. Keep out of the ways of evil

Conclusion:
   Fatherly advice is offered in the interest of helping you. This is a tremendously, helpful chapter filled with the most practical of wisdom. A wise son will heed the instruction of a wise father.

The Perfect Crime

2 SAMUEL 11

Introduction:

If you like mystery stories, etc., you have run across the idea of the perfect crime. The ultimate perfect crime has not yet been invented, but there was a man who thought he had done so. We can learn so much from him.

I.   **The Study — 2 Samuel 11**
      A. David's lust is described (vv. 1-3)
      B. David's sin is described (vv. 4-5)
      C. David's cover is detailed (vv. 6-17)
         1. First attempt — (get Uriah to stay with his wife)
         2. Second attempt — (get him drunk)
         3. Third attempt — (pre-arranged murder)
      D. David's success — he got Uriah out of the way

II.   **The Exposure**
      A. Only three people knew — none would talk
      B. God knew (last phrase of verse 27)
      C. God's revelation (2 Samuel 12)
         1. God told Nathan
         2. Nathan confronted David
         3. David condemned himself (vv. 5, 6)
      D. God's punishment is meted out

III. **The Lessons**
      A. You may do wrong and set up clever ways to hide it
      B. God always knows what you are doing
      C. God will deal with the matter
         1. He will expose you and your sin
         2. You will reap what you have sown

Conclusion:

There is no such thing as a perfect crime when it comes to God. Every crime has a witness — God Himself. Whatever secret sin you are harboring (and that is bothering you with its guilt), you might as well deal with it before God does.

Good to the Last Drop

PHILIPPIANS 3:13, 14

Introduction:
The time just before a goal is always a dangerous one. It is very hard to be in school during the spring; the last week on a job is very hard, etc. We need to be alert to the danger of any ending time, so that we can guard against the pitfalls that wait to catch us.

I. **What Is It?**
    The Tendency to Quit Before It Is Over
    A. Tempting factors — weather, weariness, love, etc.
    B. Forms it takes — grades, homework, jobs, etc.

II. **Why Is It Bad?**
    A. It can ruin much else
    B. It is usually the result of emotions getting in control
    C. It can influence future performance

III. **What Should We Do About It?**
    A. Go on as if nothing were happening
       1. Keep your mind on your work
       2. Do what needs to be done
    B. Finish everything you have to do

IV. **How Can I Help It?**
    A. Recognize it as a test of character
    B. Resolve to follow through
    C. Make completion your goal
    D. Start promptly to do what you have to do
       1. You can help others
       2. You can have free time later (do your work first — reward yourself for completion)
    E. Determine your own course (do not let others lead you)
    F. Take more interest in your work
    G. Do things one at a time

Conclusion:
It is ever so hard to "hang in there;" but it is really worth all the effort it takes. Do not lose for a few minutes, days or months what has taken so long to build and what will have such long-lasting results.

Look Out Below!!!

PROVERBS 16:18, 19

Introduction:

Teens have many problems: immorality, rock music, theft, profanity, rebellion, disobedience, etc. Which is the worst? Probably none of these. The worst is pride, and the Bible has a clear message concerning it.

I. **What Is Pride?**
  A. Excessive self-concern
  B. An excessively high impression of self
     1. Being impressed with your own importance
     2. Having a hang-up with your rights and how people treat you
  C. Thinking you are something when you are not
     1. Overstating your abilities in any area
     2. Assuming you do things well when really you do not

II. **What Causes It?**
  A. The "small pond" syndrome — you may be the best there is in your small situation but a nothing in a larger situation
  B. Your worshipful mommy and daddy who really think you are perfect — you know they do and work it for all you are worth
  C. A small amount of ability — can be deadly when you are the only one with ability in that area

III. **What Does It Do?**
  A. It blinds you — you do not see what you really are, and you do not see what you are doing and failing to do
  B. It makes you obnoxious — you get to be the kind of person others do not want to be around (either from haughtiness or from bragging)
  C. It destroys spiritual reality — you become a little, molded plastic figurine. You can not really see or know what God is trying to do in your life, because you are too busy with yourself

D. It sets you up for falls: God has a way of humiliating those whom He sees as being too proud. Watch for the fall — it is coming.

IV. **What Can Be Done About It?**
   A. Recognize it — get help if you can not see
   B. Confess it to God as sin
   C. Pray for the Holy Spirit's help
   D. Look at the entire Bible to see what you should be
   E. Ask someone else to help you (someone more mature than you are). Do not just be what your mommy or daddy think you should be.

Conclusion:

Beware of pride, for it is deadly. Read Proverbs 8:13; 11:2; 13:10; 29:23.

You had better repent of your pride.

True Confession

1 JOHN 1:4

Introduction:
The Bible calls for the confession of sin. This often bothers people, because it appears to be too easy. The truth of the matter is that it is too easy the way it is often done. Consider a number of types of confession and the motives behind them.

I.   **"I Am Suffering the Consequences and Want Out"**
      A. Confession to get relieved
      B. This was the problem of Judas

II.   **"I Do Not Want the Consequences"**
      A. I have done wrong
      B. I have done so knowing I could always ask for help

III. **"I Can Always Ask for Forgiveness"**
      A. I know I should not sin
      B. But I know God will forgive me

IV.   **"I Need My Guilt Cared for"**
      A. It comes after sin
      B. I need to have my burden lifted

V.   **"I Go Through the Motions"**
      A. I know I must confess
      B. I must get it over with ("Now I lay me down to sleep")

VI.   **"I Will Do It God's Way"**
      A. Confession = seeing it God's way
         1. Admitting it as wrong
         2. Recognizing its harm
            a. To God
            b. To me
         3. Being ashamed (repenting)
         4. Determining to be done with it
         5. Replacing it with some positive thing
      B. Guaranteed to get results

Conclusion:

Each of us needs forgiveness — frequently. God is always interested in granting the forgiveness we need. It must be sought and found His way, or there is none.

Wise Guy Or Wise Man?

PROVERBS 1:5

Introduction:
There is one in every school group. He is a "know-it-all," a "smart mouth," a guy with an inflated attitude. An earlier generation said, "Are you wise or otherwise?" The Bible condemns a wise guy but commends a wise man. Which are you? What distinguishes a wise man?

I.   **"He Will Hear and Increase Learning"**
     (He is always learning from everyone and in all situations)
     A. Keeps his prejudices and presuppositions under control
     B. Listens to the viewpoints of others
     C. Learns from every situation
        1. What someone does better than he does
        2. The mistakes and poor examples of others
        3. His own mistakes and failures
     D. Seeks new avenues of learning
        1. Always listening
        2. Reading everything possible
        3. Asking questions

II. **"He Shall Attain Unto Wise Counsels"**
     (He seeks help from wise people)
     A. Obedience to the Bible
        1. Wisest of the Wise
        2. The "wise guy" will try to outsmart authorities at times, but he never will outsmart the Bible
     B. Turning to the Bible in times of trouble
     C. Seeking and accepting counsel from the right people
        1. Spiritual authorities
        2. Those who tell us what we need rather than what we want
     D. Learning from the lives of others

Conclusion:
The Bible makes it very plain how we can distinguish between the wise and the foolish man. We can tell what others are. We can tell what we are. Are you wise or otherwise?

The Ultimate Lie

ACTS 5:1-11

Introduction:

Lying is a very common thing among teens. Almost everyone lies at times, but most would stop short of lying to God. The problem is that there are many ways in which we can lie to God, and it is very common to do so.

I. **We Lie to God, When We Go Against What We Really Believe**
   A. We all believe certain things
   B. But our conduct is not always determined by our beliefs
      1. We do what we like or feel like
      2. We mentally adjust our beliefs
   C. Thus we are not true to ourselves
   D. A man who is not true to himself is not true to God

II. **We Lie to God, When We Go Against Our Commitments**
   A. We make great commitments
   B. Then we violate them
      1. We make them knowing we will break them
      2. We break them knowing we are doing so
   C. A man who is not true to his word is not true to his God

III. **We Lie to God, When We Accept What God Says and Then Do What We Want**
   A. We listen to teaching/preaching
   B. We raise no valid objection (based on the Word)
   C. We go and do what we want to do anyhow
   D. This involves setting our wills against God's
   E. A man who will not obey God's Word is not true to his God

Conclusion:

When it comes to truth, some teens have unspeakably bad records. A man who is not even true to himself will never amount to anything for God.

In the Days of Thy Youth

2 TIMOTHY 2:23; 1 TIMOTHY 4:12; ECCLESIASTES 12:1

Introduction:
The Bible is the oldest youth book and youngest old book.
It speaks of young people: Samuel, David, Joseph and Daniel.
It also speaks to young people. Let's see what is says to young
people today.

I.   **There Are Special Problems of Youth (2 Timothy 2:23)**
   A. Every age group has its special sins (detail some)
   B. Youth seems more prone to certain things
      1. Sins of action
      2. Sins of impetuosity
      3. Sins of inexperience
   C. Paul says to run away from them
      1. Joseph — the example
      2. You are to win!

II.   **There Is a Special Potential in Youth (1 Timothy 4:12)**
   A. Do not let man look down on you as a youth
   B. Be an example to believers
      1. Reverses the usual trend
      2. It is possible for it is commanded
   C. Areas involved
      1. "Word" — what you say
      2. "Conversation" — your general conduct
      3. "Love" — the way you show what you are
      4. "Spirit" — not Holy Spirit — refers to your
         attitude
      5. "Faith" — belief in God's ability
      6. "Purity" — especially moral
         What kind of example are you?

III.   **There Is a Special Challenge to Youth (Ecclesiastes 12:1)**
   A. Remember the Creator
      1. Hold God in mind
      2. Give attention to
         a. His will
         b. His glory
         c. His purposes

B. Remember Him *now*
   1. While you are still young
   2. At the present moment
C. Remember before it is too late and
   1. Patterns are established
   2. You reap what you have sown
   3. Change becomes too difficult

Conclusion:

The teen years are such a crucial time, and the young adult years are equally important. Use them wisely. Get away from sin; establish a firm example; give attention to God and give Him the proper place in your life.